BAKE

GW00657899

Bakewell S

By Louise Maskill
Photography by Mark Titterton

BAKEWELL

Bakewell is a gem. It is the only market town within the Peak District National Park, and as such it is a bustling and popular destination for locals and tourists alike. There has been a settlement on this beautiful spot on the River Wye since Anglo-Saxon times, and since 1254 the town has grown around its market which is still held weekly on Mondays. Bakewell's beautiful courtyards, ancient bridge, industrial and agricultural heritage and huge variety of independent shops, accommodation and places to eat make it an ideal centre for your visit to the local area. This guide will help you to explore the town, give you some pointers for places to visit and things to do, and provide some local information to assist you during your visit. Welcome to Bakewell!

ABOVE: Bakewell's medieval road bridge

Foot bridge spanning the River Wye

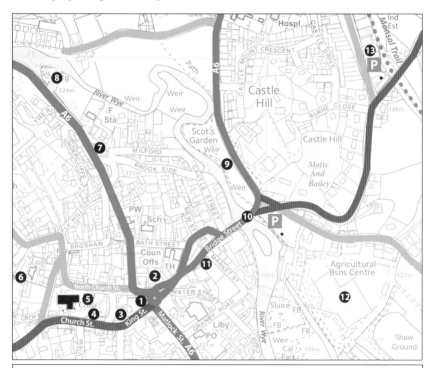

KEY

1. Rutland Arms Hotel	5. Church of All Saints	9. Scott's Garden	12. Agricultural Business
2. Bath Gardens	6. Old House Museum	10. Medieval bridge	Centre
3. Old Town Hall	7. Victoria Mill	11. Old Market Hall &	13. Monsal Trail
4. Almshouses	8. Holme Bridge	Visitor Centre	

A STROLL AROUND THE TOWN

Bakewell is a small town which is easy to explore on foot, and there is much to discover. If you wish you can follow this section as a guided walk around the town and its immediate environs, starting at the Rutland Arms in the centre of the town, but equally you could wander as you please and look things up as you come across them. Either way, Bakewell will be sure to delight and interest you.

Rutland Square and the Rutland Arms Hotel At the heart of Bakewell is Rutland Square, overlooked by the elegant Rutland Arms Hotel. The layout of this part of the town was created in the early nineteenth century when the Duke of Rutland decided to capitalise on the spa town tourism that was bringing visitors to the area. The Rutland Arms was built on the site of the Old White Horse coaching inn, and since it opened in 1804 it has played host to many famous names, including Lord Byron, Jane Austen, Charles Dickens and of course the Dukes of Rutland and Devonshire.

The Rutland Arms Hotel as seen from Bath Gardens

Bath Gardens Also overlooking Rutland Square, these gardens are the last vestiges of Bakewell's attempt to become a spa resort. Thermal waters bubble up through a fountain in the gardens, and the site used to contain an elaborate bathing complex built by the Duke of Rutland. The bath house still stands, but the waters are somewhat chilly compared to the warmer waters of rival towns such as Matlock Bath and Buxton, and Bakewell Spa never really took off.

The Old Town Hall Heading up King Street from Rutland Square (to the left of the Rutland Arms) you arrive at the Old Town Hall, which has had a succession of uses since it was built in 1602. As well as being the first Town Hall, among other things it has served as a hospital, a butter market, a court, a school, a working men's club and a fire station. Behind it stand the town's historic almshouses, built in 1709 to give shelter to destitute townsfolk and recently restored to provide affordable housing.

TOP: Bath Gardens ABOVE: King's Court
OPPOSITE PAGE TOP: The Old Town Hall BOTTOM: Almshouses

The Church of All Saints At the top of the hill and dominating the skyline of the town is the imposing Church of All Saints, with its unusual octagonal spire. The majority of the fabric of the building dates from the thirteenth and fourteenth centuries, but it contains fragments of Saxon and Norman architecture and is thought to have developed from a much earlier structure. There are the remains of two Saxon crosses in the churchyard. Inside, the Vernon chapel contains the tombs of the Vernon family, ancestors of the Dukes of Rutland, and on the south wall of the church there is a rare and beautiful fourteenth century alabaster monument to Godfrey and Avena de Foljambe.

ABOVE: Church of All Saints
OPPOSITE PAGE: Memorial to Sir George Manners and family

Old House Museum Across Church Lane behind the church is the Old House Museum. Originally built in 1534 by a member of the local Gell family to house his tax collector, down the years the building has been extended and converted many times. Ending up as a row of mill workers' cottages, it was saved from demolition in the 1950s by the Bakewell Historical Society and now houses a museum with historical tableaus, textile displays, and lots of information about the fascinating architecture of the building.

TOP: Victoria Mill

ABOVE: Scott's Garden riverside meadow

Victoria Mill Head down the steep Fly Hill towards Buxton Road and turn left, walking a short distance to pass Victoria Mill on the right. Since Saxon times a corn mill has stood on this site; the present building dates from the late eighteenth and early nineteenth centuries and is now apartments, but the mill wheel that once harnessed the River Wye to power the machinery can still be seen in the yard.

Holme Bridge Continue along Buxton Road past the Fire Station and turn right to reach Holme Bridge. This narrow eighteenth century packhorse bridge crosses the River Wye just outside the town, built so that packhorse trains could cross the river without paying tolls in the centre of town. Over the bridge, turn right along Holme Lane to a path through the riverside meadow known as Scott's Garden; turn right across the meadow to come back towards the town.

Bridge Street The footpath from Scott's Garden meets the Baslow Road; turn right to cross the beautiful fourteenth century road bridge with its five Gothic arches. Dating from around 1200, it is one of the oldest medieval bridges in the country that still carries a main road, coping amazingly well with twentieth century traffic. It is a Scheduled Ancient Monument, and provides a wonderful view of the River Wye flowing serenely beneath.

Old Market Hall A short distance along Bridge Street is the seventeenth century Old Market Hall. This building was originally open-sided, and has functioned as a wash house, a dance hall and a library. It now houses the Bakewell Visitor Centre, hosting exhibitions and providing a wealth of information about the town and the local area.

Market and Shopping Area Back in the town centre, take some time to browse the huge variety of shops that Bakewell has to offer, ranging from crafts and arts to books, outdoor equipment and clothing. If you happen to be in Bakewell on a Monday, visit the regular market which has been held in the town since a Royal Charter was granted in 1330. It is the only regular market in the Peak District National Park, hosting over 150 stalls and welcoming many thousands of locals and visitors each year.

When you have wandered around the shops, make your way back to Rutland Square and the starting point of your stroll round one of Derbyshire's most vibrant, bustling and popular market towns. Treat yourself to lunch or afternoon tea in the Rutland Arms, or rest your legs on one of the benches in the Bath Gardens – recharge your batteries, because there's plenty more to discover!

TOP: Holme Bridge
MIDDLE: Market stalls
BOTTOM: Bakewell
Delhi, Buxton Road

ANNUAL EVENTS

The Bakewell Agricultural Show Known locally as the Little Royal, the Bakewell Agricultural Show is held at the Bakewell Showground just outside town on the first Wednesday and Thursday in August each year. Organised by the Bakewell Agricultural and Horticultural Society, the show is one of the largest covered agricultural shows in the UK, attracting around 70,000 visitors over its two days. It features events and attractions for all the family, from livestock and equestrian events to artisan food producers, craftspeople and horticulture displays.

Bakewell Well Dressing The peculiarly Derbyshire custom of well dressing involves decorating wells, springs or other communal water sources with pictures made of petals, leaves and other natural objects pressed into clay panels. In Bakewell the ancient custom was revived in 1971 after dying out in the eighteenth century; there are a number of well dressings around the town, with the event taking place over a week in late June and early July.

Bakewell Carnival takes place on the last weekend of Well Dressing Week and involves the whole town. There is a procession of floats through the town centre, and the crowning of the Carnival Queen. Marching bands accompany them through the town to the fête at the Agricultural Centre, and there are various races, games and stalls – fun for all the family!

TOP & MIDDLE: The Bakewell Agricultural Show
BOTTOM: Well dressing

OTHER LOCAL ATTRACTIONS

Thornbridge Brewery Ten minutes' walk from the heart of Bakewell along the Buxton Road is the multi-award-winning Thornbridge Brewery, established in 2005 and now brewing a wide variety of cask, keg and bottled beers. Tours of the brewery are run on Wednesdays and Fridays, with an introduction to the brewing process and the opportunity to sample some of the beers in a souvenir branded glass, which will be yours to take home.

Agricultural Business Centre Hosts a monthly Farmers' Market (on the last Saturday of every month) and has been a huge success since its inception in 1998. It regularly attracts more than 5000 visitors, and there is a long list of traders waiting for the chance to run one of the seventy or so stalls. There are some local crafts represented, but the vast majority of stalls are dedicated to local and traceable food and drink. There is also a weekly cattle auction held on Mondays, where members of the public may come along and watch the sales, but be careful not to wave or you could be going home with more than you bargained for!

Bakewell's weekly cattle auction at the Agricultural Business Centre

TOP: Chatsworth House
ABOVE: The Long Gallery,
Haddon Hall

Chatsworth House and Gardens

Slightly further afield, Chatsworth House is just over three miles from Bakewell, and has been the seat of the Dukes of Devonshire and home to the Cavendish family since Tudor times. Known as the Palace of the Peak, the house is stunning inside and out and is set in parkland and gardens which owe much to the influence of Joseph Paxton, who was head gardener at Chatsworth in the nineteenth century. With a children's farm and adventure play area, well-stocked gift-shops and a variety of places to eat, Chatsworth is entertaining for all the family and is well worth a visit at any time of the year – the Christmas decorations in the house are especially magical, or you could time your visit to coincide with the annual Chatsworth Country Fair in September.

Haddon Hall Closer to Bakewell, less flamboyant than Chatsworth but equally enchanting is Haddon Hall. Nestling on the banks of the River Wye, Haddon is one of the seats of the Dukes of Rutland, inhabited by the Vernon and Manners families since the thirteenth century. The house is medieval and Tudor in style, and has featured in many television and film productions including The Princess Bride (1986), Pride and Prejudice (2006) and two versions of Jane Eyre (1996 and 2006). It has its own romantic tale involving the elopement of Dorothy Vernon and John Manners during a ball in 1563 – there is even an opera telling the tale named after the hall!

Lathkill Dale One of the most beautiful dales in the Peak District, Lathkill Dale was formed by the River Lathkill as it rises from springs near Monyash, west of Bakewell, flowing down a steep-sided valley for just over six miles until it meets the River Wye. The water is pure and clear, and brown trout can be clearly seen in the fishing ponds. Dippers and water voles also make the dale their home, and the upper reaches are designated a Site of Special Scientific Interest. The dale is popular with tourists and walkers alike, with access from car parks at Conksbury Bridge, Over Haddon, Youlgreave and Moor Lane. The Lathkill Inn at Over Haddon is also well worth a visit!

Caudwell's Mill was built in 1874 and is a working flour mill that has been run by a charitable trust for the last forty years. It operates daily, and the shop sells flour and oat goods and baked products. The complex also includes craft shops, a forge, galleries and a café.

Peak Shopping Village, Rowsley a few miles from Bakewell, there are over 20 retailers, ranging from fashion, sportswear and luggage to local produce, gifts and books. The shopping centre offers free parking, and there are regular events such as tea dances.

Peak Rail Running from Rowsley to Matlock, Peak Rail is a a fabulous day out for all rail enthusiasts. The railway operates a steam and heritage diesel service; as well as taking a nostalgic trip on one of the restored trains you can visit the museum which tells the story of the Midland Railway. There are opportunities to shop and eat, and there are even plans to extend the line from Rowsley as far as Bakewell, involving the restoration of the Haddon Tunnel and the Coombs Road viaduct.

MONSAL TRAIL & HASSOP STATION

Venturing further out of the town centre, the Monsal Trail provides an excellent and easy way to walk, cycle or ride through the Derbyshire countryside. The trail itself is an 8.5-mile stretch of converted railway line starting in Wye Dale and ending at Coombs Road in Bakewell, offering spectacular off-road cycling and walking through lit tunnels and across the famous Headstone Viaduct at Monsal Head. There are information panels explaining the former history of the route, and the trail forms part of a wider network of trails and pathways stretching across the Peak District. Don't miss the café and bookshop at Hassop Station, a short distance from Bakewell along the trail, and the Monsal Head Hotel also provides an excellent refreshment stop with stunning views across Monsal Dale.

BAKEWELL PUDDINGS

Of course, no visit to Bakewell would be complete without sampling the world-famous Bakewell pudding (not to be confused with the much inferior Bakewell tart – make this mistake at your peril!). The dessert consists of a flaky pastry base spread with jam and then topped with an egg and almond topping and baked until the almond custard sets.

There are several stories explaining the origin of this dessert, and a number of shops in Bakewell claim to hold the original recipe – the most usual story is that it was first made by accident by a cook working at the Old White Horse Inn, which once occupied the site where the Rutland Arms now stands. Mrs Greaves, the landlady, left instructions for a kitchen maid to make a strawberry tart for a visiting nobleman, but instead of stirring the egg and almond mixture into the pastry, the girl spread it on top of the jam. The result was an immediate success, and a local legend was born.

There are several shops offering this teatime treat, each with their own jealously guarded secret recipe and all delicious – but they do sell out, so make sure you pick one up. Eat the pudding warm or cold – it's a delicious luxurious treat. Don't leave Bakewell without a taste of a genuine Bakewell pudding; you'll never go back to tarts again!

LOCAL AMENITIES/USEFUL INFORMATION

Tourist Information
The Bakewell Visitor Centre is located in the Old Market Hall in the centre of town.

Contact details:
☎ 01629 816558
Email: bakewell@peakdistrict.gov.uk
www.peakdistrict.gov.uk/visiting/visitor-centres/bakewell

Public Toilets
There are public toilets at the Agricultural Business Centre, on Granby Road, at the Recreation Ground and on Granby Road next to Boots. All are open year-round, and are free to use with disabled access, and all except Riverside have baby changing facilities.

Getting Around by Public Transport
Bakewell is well served by bus routes to and from most of the popular tourist attractions in the local area. Among other destinations, local buses run to Chatsworth, Buxton, Castleton and Monsal Head, Eyam, Lathkill Dale and Matlock Bath, and there are direct services to Sheffield, Chesterfield, Derby and Manchester. The Visitor Centre will be able to provide up-to-date timetable information, or visit one of the websites below to help you plan your travel.

www.derbyshire.gov.uk/buses
www.peakdistrict.gov.uk/visiting/publictransport

Cycling is a viable and popular way to explore the beautiful Peak District, and Bakewell is ideally placed as a base because of the Monsal Trail, an 8.5-mile stretch of converted railway line which runs past Bakewell and takes in some of the most stunning local scenery as well as tunnels and the famous Headstone Viaduct. You can hire bicycles if you don't have your own; the website below contains plenty of information, or contact the Bakewell Visitor Centre.

www.peakdistrict.gov.uk/visiting/cycle

Sports and Leisure Facilities
Many people visit the Peak District simply to walk or cycle, but if you would like to swim, visit Bakewell Swimming Pool off Granby Road, or you could take in a round of golf at Bakewell Golf Club on Station Road.

www.derbyshiredales.gov.uk/leisure-a-culture/leisure-centres/bakewell-swimming-pool

www.bakewellgolfclub.co.uk

Medical and Health Care

Bakewell Medical Centre is located on Butts Road, operating a traditional GP practice.

The closest Accident and Emergency department is at Chesterfield and North Derbyshire Royal Hospital at Calow, near Chesterfield.

There are two dental practices in town, and two pharmacies offering prescription services as well as general pharmacy advice.

Contact details:

Bakewell Medical Centre
Butts Road ☎ 01629 816636

Chesterfield and North Derbyshire
Royal Hospital
Calow, S44 5BL ☎ 01246 277271

Boots the Chemist Ltd
Granby Road, ☎ 01629 812043

Lloyd's the Chemists
Matlock Street ☎ 01629 813215

Diamond Court Dental Practice
Water Street,☎ 01629 812991

Smith's Dental Surgery
Granby Road ☎ 01629 812066

Published by Bradwell Books
9 Orgreave Close Sheffield S13 9NP
Email – books@bradwellbooks.co.uk
A CIP catalogue record for this book is available from the British Library.
1st Edition

ISBN – 9781910551608

Print – Gomer Press, Llandysul, Ceredigion SA44 4JL

Text by – Louise Maskill
Design by – Andy Caffrey
Typeset by – Mark Titterton
Photography by - Mark Titterton
Photography © Mark Titterton 2015

FRONT COVER: Bridge Street from The Rutland Arms Hotel
BACK COVER LEFT Bath Gardens MIDDLE: Traditional Bakewell Puddings
RIGHT: River Wye BOTTOM: Heavy horse turnout at the Bakewell Show